The Goulash Recipe Book

Discover Many Different Ways to Cook Warm Goulash!

BY: Allie Allen

COOK & ENJOY

Copyright 2019 Allie Allen

Copyright Notes

This book is written as an informational tool. While the author has taken every precaution to ensure the accuracy of the information provided therein, the reader is warned that they assume all risk when following the content. The author will not be held responsible for any damages that may occur as a result of the readers' actions.

The author does not give permission to reproduce this book in any form, including but not limited to: print, social media posts, electronic copies or photocopies, unless permission is expressly given in writing.

Table of Contents

Introduction 6

    Classic Hungarian Goulash 7

    German Goulash 9

    Persian Goulash 12

    White Bean and Beef Goulash 15

    Low-Carb Beef Goulash 17

    Spiced Armenian Lamb Goulash 19

    Beef Goulash with Parsnips and Raisins 22

    American Goulash 25

    Lamb Goulash with Parsnips 28

    Hungarian Lamb Goulash 31

    Bell Pepper Goulash Soup 33

    German Lamb Goulash 35

    Goulash with Sour Cream and Yogurt 38

Crockpot Hungarian Goulash 41

Goulash Casserole 44

Thick Beef and Baby Onion Goulash 46

Chili Goulash 49

Polish Goulash 52

North African Fish Goulash 54

Egyptian Goulash 57

Lamb Zucchini Goulash 60

Chickpea Goulash 63

Crockpot Vegan Goulash 65

Viennese Goulash 67

Low-Carb Lamb Goulash 69

Chicken Goulash 71

Texan Goulash 74

One-Pot Goulash 77

Ground Lamb Goulash 79

Sweet Potato Goulash Soup 82

Conclusion 84

About the Author 85

Author's Afterthoughts 87

Introduction

Looking for a change in your usual selection of recipes? Want to put up something warming and hearty? If your answer is yes, then this book is for you! With 30 delicious goulash recipes, you'll be able to put up a dish that's filling, warm and absolutely delicious!

All of the recipes in here are detailed and come with step-by-step instructions, and so can be made by even the most beginner cook! Plus all the recipes can be easily doubled or even tripled! So what are you waiting for? Let's get started!

Classic Hungarian Goulash

A classic and delicious Hungarian goulash recipe with paprika and broth.

Makes: 12 servings

Prep: 30 mins

Cook: 1 hr. 30 mins

Ingredients:

- 4 onions
- ½ tsp. pepper
- 4 tsp. lard
- 4 tbsp. paprika
- 2 tsp. caraway seeds
- ½ cup flour
- 4 cups beef broth
- 1 lb. stewing beef & cut into one inch cubes
- 2 cups diced tomatoes
- 2 tsp. salt

Directions:

In a big pot, melt the lard. Add in the onion and cook for 3 mins. Add in the seeds & paprika.

In a big bowl, mix the beef with some flour. Add it to the pot and cook for 4 mins. Add in a bit of broth to remove the brown bit from the bottom of the pot & then add in the remaining. Add in the tomatoes and seasoning. Bring to boil and then cover & simmer for 2 hrs. or until meat is tender.

Serve.

German Goulash

You don't need to spend too long dealing with difficult recipes to make a great dinner. German goulash is a favorite meal for many families. It's made with macaroni, ground beef and veggies, and it's quite hearty.

Makes: 6 Servings

Prep: 10 mins

Cook: 15 mins

Ingredients:

- 1 1/2 cup of macaroni, uncooked
- 1 1/4 cup of cheddar cheese, cubed
- 1 x 2 1/4-ounce can of olives, sliced
- 2 x 15-ounce cans of tomatoes, fire-roasted
- 1 tsp. of salt, seasoned
- 1 tsp. of pepper, ground
- 2 tsp. of oregano
- 2 diced celery stalks
- 3 minced garlic cloves
- 1 diced medium onion, yellow
- 1 pound ground beef, lean
- 1 tsp. of oil, vegetable

Directions:

Heat oil in skillet on med-high. Add celery, garlic, onion and ground beef. Cook 'til ground beef has cooked through. Use wooden spoon to scrape up any pieces from pan bottom.

Season using black pepper, seasoned salt and oregano. Add sliced olives and tomatoes. Reduce heat. Simmer on low for 15 mins.

Cook macaroni in pot of lightly salted water until it is al dente. Set aside after draining well.

Add cheese to skillet. Allow to melt for several minutes. Add macaroni. Combine well. Let the meal simmer for five more minutes. Serve hot.

Persian Goulash

Mouth-watering Persian beef stew recipe with cinnamon and beans.

Makes: 6 servings

Prep: 10 mins

Cook: 1 hr. 35 mins

Ingredients:

- One lb. lean stew beef, cut into cubes
- 3 tbsp. olive oil, divided
- Salt and black pepper
- 2 tsp. turmeric
- 1/2 onion, chopped
- 1/2 tsp. cinnamon
- 6 tbsp. fresh parsley, chopped
- 2 1/2 cups. water
- 3 tbsp. chives
- 1 lemon, juice of
- 2 tsp. ground cumin
- 1 tbsp. flour
- 1 cans kidney beans, drained & rinsed

Directions:

Place a large pan over medium heat. Heat 2 tablespoons of olive oil in it. Brown in it the stew meat for 12 min.

Stir in the cumin, turmeric and cinnamon. Cook them for 2 min. Pour in the water and cook them until they start boiling.

Put on the lid and cook them for 48 min while stirring from to time.

Place a small skillet over medium heat. Heat 1 tablespoon of oil in it. Add the parsley with chives. Cook them for 3 min. Stir them into the beef stew with beans and lemon juice.

Sprinkle some salt and pepper on the stew then add to it 1 tablespoon of flour. Cook the stew for 35 min until it thickens. Serve it warm.

White Bean and Beef Goulash

A delicious goulash recipe with beans and potatoes.

Makes: 6 servings

Prep: 20 mins

Cook: 1 hr. 15 mins

Ingredients:

- 2 tbsp. olive oil
- 4 cups lean stew beef cubes
- 2 medium-size onions, chopped
- 4 cloves garlic, minced
- 4 cups (1 quart) low-sodium beef broth
- 1 cup canned white beans, rinsed and drained
- 2 cups diced, peeled potatoes, cut ½ inch thick
- 3 carrots, peeled and cut into 1-inch pieces
- 1 tbsp. fresh rosemary, crushed (optional)
- 1 bay leaf
- Salt and freshly ground black pepper

Directions:

Place the olive oil in a large heavy soup pot over med-high heat. Working in batches, add the beef cubes and brown well on all sides, 4 to 5 minutes. Set the browned beef aside.

Reduce the heat to medium. Add the onions & garlic to the pot and cook, stirring, until they just begin to brown, about 3 minutes. Add the beef broth and let it come to a simmer, scraping the bottom of the pan to loosen the cooked bits of beef. Add the reserved beef, white beans, potatoes, carrots, rosemary, and bay leaf. Cover & reduce the heat to low. Let the simmer until beef is cooked through and tender, about 1 hour. The stew can be refrigerated for 3 or 4 days.

Before serving, taste for seasoning adding salt and pepper to taste and remove and discard the bay leaf.

Low-Carb Beef Goulash

Delicious low-carb beef goulash with zucchini and beef.

Makes: 4 servings

Prep: 5 mins

Cook: 35 mins

Ingredients:

- 1 lb. stewing beef cubes
- Salt and pepper
- 2 tbsp. olive oil
- 1 onion, chopped finely
- 1 garlic clove, chopped finely
- 14 oz. canned tomatoes in juice
- ½ tsp. paprika
- 9 oz. zucchini, sliced
- 2 tbsp. chopped fresh thyme

Directions:

Season the beef with pepper. Heat the oil in a flameproof casserole. Add in the onion and garlic. Cook for 5 minutes or until softened. Add the beef & cook.

Add the tomatoes with their juice, paprika, thyme and salt.

Boil and then simmer for 30 mins. stirring occasionally and turning the beef once during cooking, until the beef and zucchini are tender.

Serve hot.

Spiced Armenian Lamb Goulash

A delicious Armenian lamb goulash recipe.

Makes: 4 servings

Prep: 10 mins

Cook: 1 hr. 10 mins

Ingredients:

- 2 tbsp. butter
- 1 large yellow onion, peeled and diced
- 2 lb. lean, boneless leg of lamb, cubed
- 1/2 tsp. paprika
- 1/2 tsp. freshly ground black pepper
- 1/2 tsp. ground allspice
- 1/4 tsp. ground cinnamon
- Salt to taste
- 1/4 cup tomato paste
- 1 cup water

Directions:

Dissolve the butter in a 6-quart Dutch oven and bring to temperature over medium heat. Add the onions and sauté 3 minutes.

Put the onions to the side, add the lamb, and brown the meat in the butter. Mix the paprika, pepper, allspice, and cinnamon into the meat and onions. Add salt to taste.

Put the meat and onions to the side and sauté the tomato paste 2 minutes, then stir it into the meat and onions. Slowly pour the water into the pan. Stir. Bring to a boil, & then reduce, cover, & simmer 45 minutes or until the meat is tender.

Cover, and simmer 15 more minutes.

Serve.

Beef Goulash with Parsnips and Raisins

Beef goulash recipe with parsnips, carrots and raisins for sweetness.

Makes: 6 servings

Prep: 10 mins

Cook: 10 hrs.

Ingredients:

Serves : 4–6

- 2 tbsp. vegetable oil
- 2 tbsp. all-purpose flour
- 1 (1 1/2-pound) beef chuck roast, cut into 1" cubes
- 1 (1-pound) bag baby carrots
- 2 large parsnips, peeled and sliced into 1/2" pieces
- 1 large yellow onion, peeled & roughly chopped
- 1 (14.5-ounce) can diced tomatoes, undrained
- 1 (14-ounce) can beef broth
- 2 cloves garlic, minced
- 1 bay leaf
- 1 tsp. dried thyme, crushed
- 1/4 tsp. freshly ground black pepper
- 1/2 cup almond- or pimiento-stuffed green olives
- 1/3 cup golden raisins

Directions:

Add the oil to a 4-quart slow cooker and bring to temperature over high heat. Toss the meat in the flour. Add half of the meat to the slow cooker and sauté until brown; push the meat to the side and add remaining meat, stirring to coat all the meat in the hot oil. Wipe out any excess fat.

Add the carrots, parsnips, onion, tomatoes, broth, garlic, bay leaf, thyme, and pepper to the cooker; stir to combine. Reduce heat to low; cover & cook 8–10 hours.

Remove and discard the bay leaf. Stir in the olives and raisins. Serve warm.

American Goulash

A delicious American twist on Goulash.

Makes: 16 servings

Prep: 10 mins

Cook: 30 mins

Ingredients:

- 2 cups sharp shredded cheddar cheese
- 4 lb. ground beef
- 6 ½ cup water
- 2 onions
- 8 cloves of garlic, minced
- 4 cans tomato sauce
- 2 tbsp. beef bullion
- 4 cans diced tomato
- 6 bay leaves
- 2 tbsp. Italian seasoning
- 6 tbsp. soy sauce
- 2 tbsp. salt
- 2 tsp. paprika
- 1 tsp. black pepper
- 4 cups elbow macaroni pasta uncooked
- Parsley, to serve

Directions:

In a big pot, brown the beef. Remove & drain.

Add onion & cook over med heat for 7 mins. Add the garlic & cook for 2 mins.

Bring the beef back in and add the water, bouillon, tomatoes, bay leaves, soy sauce and seasonings. Bring to boil, reduce, cover & simmer for 25 mins.

Add in the elbow pasta, cover & simmer for 20 mins or until cooked.

Add in the cheese, stir and then serve with parsley.

Lamb Goulash with Parsnips

A delicious lamb roast goulash recipe with parsnips.

Makes: 6 servings

Prep: 10 mins

Cook: 10 hrs.

Ingredients:

Serves: 4–6

- 2 tbsp. vegetable oil
- 2 tbsp. all-purpose flour
- 1 (1 1/2-pound) lamb chuck roast, cut into 1" cubes
- 1 (1-pound) bag baby carrots
- 2 large parsnips, peeled and sliced into 1/2" pieces
- 1 large yellow onion, peeled & roughly chopped
- 1 (14.5-ounce) can diced tomatoes, undrained
- 1 (14-ounce) can beef broth
- 2 cloves garlic, minced
- 1 bay leaf
- 1 tsp. dried thyme, crushed
- 1/4 tsp. freshly ground black pepper
- 1/2 cup almond- or pimiento-stuffed green olives
- 1/3 cup golden raisins

Directions:

Add the oil to a 4-quart slow cooker and bring to temperature over high heat. Toss the meat in the flour. Add half of the meat to the slow cooker and sauté until brown; push the meat to the side and add remaining meat, stirring to coat all the meat in the hot oil. Wipe out any excess fat.

Add the carrots, parsnips, onion, tomatoes, broth, garlic, bay leaf, thyme, and pepper to the cooker; stir to combine. Reduce heat to low; cover & cook 8–10 hours.

Remove and discard the bay leaf. Stir in the olives and raisins. Serve warm.

Hungarian Lamb Goulash

A delicious Hungarian lamb goulash recipe with paprika and broth.

Makes: 12 servings

Prep: 30 mins

Cook: 1 hr. 30 mins

Ingredients:

- 4 onions
- ½ tsp. pepper
- 4 tsp. lard
- 4 tbsp. paprika
- 2 tsp. caraway seeds
- ½ cup flour
- 4 cups beef broth
- 1 lb. stewing lamb & cut into one inch cubes
- 2 cups diced tomatoes
- 2 tsp. salt

Directions:

In a big pot, melt the lard. Add in the onion and cook for 3 mins. Add in the seeds & paprika.

In a big bowl, mix the lamb with some flour. Add it to the pot and cook for 4 mins. Add in a bit of broth to remove the brown bit from the bottom of the pot & then add in the remaining. Add in the tomatoes and seasoning. Bring to boil and then cover & simmer for 2 hrs. or until meat is tender.

Serve.

Bell Pepper Goulash Soup

A warm and delicious goulash soup recipe with beef and bell peppers.

Makes: 4 servings

Prep: 20 mins

Cook: 1 hr.

Ingredients:

- 2 tbsp. oil
- 2 large onions, sliced
- 6 garlic cloves, sliced
- 0.8 lb. stewing beef, diced finely
- 2 tsp. caraway seeds
- 4 tsp. paprika
- 2 cans chopped tomatoes
- 4 ½ cup beef stock
- 2 bell peppers, diced

Directions:

Heat oil in a pot. Add in the onions & garlic and cook for 6 mins. Add in the beef and cook until beef is browned. Add in the seeds, paprika, stock and tomatoes and cook on low for 35 mins.

Add in the bell peppers and cook for 25 mins or until tender. Serve.

German Lamb Goulash

Delicious German goulash with macaroni, ground lamb and veggies, and it's quite hearty.

Makes: 6 Servings

Prep: 10 mins

Cook: 15 mins

Ingredients:

- 1 1/2 cup of macaroni, uncooked
- 1 1/4 cup of cheddar cheese, cubed
- 1 x 2 1/4-ounce can of olives, sliced
- 2 x 15-ounce cans of tomatoes, fire-roasted
- 1 tsp. of salt, seasoned
- 1 tsp. of pepper, ground
- 2 tsp. of oregano
- 2 diced celery stalks
- 3 minced garlic cloves
- 1 diced medium onion, yellow
- 1 pound ground lamb, lean
- 1 tsp. of oil, vegetable

Directions:

Heat oil in skillet on med-high. Add celery, garlic, onion and ground lamb. Cook 'til ground lamb has cooked through. Use wooden spoon to scrape up any pieces from pan bottom.

Season using black pepper, seasoned salt and oregano. Add sliced olives and tomatoes. Reduce heat. Simmer on low for 15 mins.

Cook macaroni in pot of lightly salted water until it is al dente. Set aside after draining well.

Add cheese to skillet. Allow to melt for several minutes. Add macaroni. Combine well. Let the meal simmer for five more minutes. Serve hot.

Goulash with Sour Cream and Yogurt

A great way to use those tough cuts of meat or to stretch a small amount for a crowd, this dish can be cooked ahead and the yogurt and sour cream added just before serving.

Makes: 6 servings

Prep: 10 mins

Cook: 1 hr.

Ingredients:

- 2 pounds stew meat or sirloin steak
- 1 tbsp. vegetable oil
- 1 cup diced onions
- 1 cup diced carrots
- One 16-ounce can tomato
- 1 cup beef stock
- 1 tbsp. paprika
- 1½ tsp. salt
- ½ tsp. pepper
- ¼ tsp. ground cloves
- 1 tbsp. brown sugar
- 2 tbsp. rice flour
- ¼ cup water
- ¼ cup sour cream
- ¼ cup plain yogurt

Directions:

Cut the stew meat into ½-inch slices (or slice the steak into ¼-inch slices). In a large skillet, brown the beef quickly. Remove the meat from the skillet, then add the oil and sauté the onion until clear.

Return the beef to the skillet. Add the carrots, tomatoes, beef stock, paprika, salt, pepper, cloves, and sugar. Combine the rice flour with the water and stir in. Cover & let simmer until the meat is tender, 20 minutes to an hour. Longer cooking seems to increase the flavor.

Just before serving, stir in the sour cream and yogurt and heat through.

Crockpot Hungarian Goulash

Delicious goulash made in the crockpot to enhance flavor!

Makes: 6 servings

Prep: 10 mins

Cook: 7 hrs.

Ingredients:

- 2 pounds stew meat or sirloin steak
- 1 tbsp. vegetable oil
- 1 cup diced onions
- 1 cup diced carrots
- One 16-ounce can tomato
- 1 cup beef stock
- 1 tbsp. paprika
- 1½ tsp. salt
- ½ tsp. pepper
- ¼ tsp. ground cloves
- 1 tbsp. brown sugar
- 2 tbsp. rice flour
- ¼ cup water
- ¼ cup sour cream
- ¼ cup plain yogurt

Directions:

Cut the stew meat into ½-inch slices (or slice the steak into ¼-inch slices). In a large skillet, brown the beef quickly. Remove the meat from the skillet, then add the oil and sauté the onion until clear.

Place it in your electric pot. Add the carrots, tomatoes, beef stock, paprika, salt, pepper, cloves, and sugar. Combine the rice flour with the water and stir in. Cover and cook for 6-7 hrs. on LOW.

Just before serving, stir in the sour cream and yogurt and heat through.

Goulash Casserole

Goulash casserole with coconut oil, carrots, peas and onions.

Makes: 6 servings

Prep: 5 mins

Cook: 2 hrs.

Ingredients:

- 1-1/2 cups chopped carrots
- 1 cup chopped onions
- 2 tbsp. coconut oil
- 1-1/2 cups green peas
- 4 cups beef stock
- 1/2 tsp. salt
- 1/2 tsp. paprika
- 1/4 tsp. ground black pepper
- 1/2 tsp. minced garlic
- 4 pounds boneless chuck roast

Directions:

Combine all of the shown above ingredients in a large casserole dish, cover, and bake for 2 hours on 400°F.

Serve.

Thick Beef and Baby Onion Goulash

A thick beef and onion goulash with spices and garlic and served with potatoes.

Makes: 6 servings

Prep: 10 mins

Cook: 1 hr. 30 mins

Ingredients:

- 2 tbsp. olive oil
- 1 lb. baby onions, peeled and left whole
- 2 garlic cloves, peeled and halved
- 1 tsp. ground cloves
- 2 lb. stewing beef, cubed
- Chopped fresh flat-leaf parsley, to garnish
- 1/2 tsp. ground cinnamon
- 2 tbsp. tomato purée
- Salt and pepper
- 4 cups beef stock
- 1/2 tsp. paprika
- Grated rind & juice of 1 orange
- 1 tsp. ground cumin
- 1 bay leaf
- Boiled/mashed potatoes, to serve

Directions:

Preheat the oven to 300°F.

Heat oil in a flameproof casserole. Add the onions & the garlic and fry for 5 mins. Add the beef and cook about 5 minutes.

Stir the cinnamon, cloves, paprika, cumin, tomato purée, salt & pepper into the casserole. Pour in the stock, stirring in any glazed bits from the bottom, then add the grated orange rind, bay leaf, and juice. Boil, then cover the casserole.

Cook for about 1 ¼ hrs. Remove the cover and cook for another hr. stirring once or twice during this time, until the meat is tender.

Garnish with parsley & serve hot.

Chili Goulash

A delicious and warming chili goulash recipe.

Makes: 6 servings

Prep: 10 min

Cook: 20 mins

Ingredients:

- 2 tbsp. vegetable oil
- 1 cup chopped yellow onion
- 2 cloves garlic, minced
- 1 lb. ground beef
- ¾ cup chopped green bell pepper
- 1 tbsp. chili powder
- ½ tsp. paprika
- ½ tsp. ground cumin
- 2 (15.25-ounce) cans kidney beans, rinsed & drained
- 1 tsp. crushed red pepper flakes
- 1 (28-ounce) can diced tomatoes
- 1 cup canned crushed tomatoes
- Sour cream, for serving
- Chopped green onions, for serving
- Grated cheddar cheese, for serving

Directions:

Warm the oil in a cast iron Dutch oven over medium heat on a grill or on a grate over a medium-heat fire. Add the onions & cook, stirring often, for 5 minutes. Add the garlic and stir. Add the ground beef, stirring to crumble the meat while it browns. After the meat browns, add the green peppers and cook for 2 minutes more. Stir in the chili powder, paprika, cumin, kidney beans, and red pepper flakes. Add the diced tomatoes with juice and the crushed tomatoes. Stir well and simmer for 15 minutes. Serve in bowls, topped with sour cream, chopped green onions, and grated cheddar cheese.

Polish Goulash

Polish-inspired goulash recipe in a crockpot.

Makes: 12 servings

Prep: 5 mins

Cook: 10 hrs.

Ingredients:

- 2 pounds boneless chuck, chopped
- 1 pound chopped cooked Polish sausage or kielbasa
- 1 large chopped onion
- 2 yellow bell peppers (seeded and chopped)
- 1 packet onion soup mix
- 4 chopped medium size tomatoes
- 1 cup beef broth
- ¼ cup tomato sauce

Directions:

In a crockpot, add in all of the ingredients. Season with salt & pepper.

Cover & cook on low for 10 hrs.

Serve.

North African Fish Goulash

A delicious North-African-inspired fish goulash recipe with bell peppers and sweet paprika.

Makes: 4 servings

Prep: 5 mins

Cook: 55 mins

Ingredients:

- ⅓ cup (80 ml) extra-virgin olive oil
- 2 red bell peppers, cut into long, thin strips
- 8 large cloves garlic, coarsely slivered
- ¼ cup (60 g) tomato paste
- 1½ cups (350 ml) water
- 3 large dried red chile peppers (New Mexico pepper works well)
- 2 tbsp. (12 g) sweet paprika
- ½ tsp. ground cumin
- 1 tbsp. (5 g) Harissa with Caraway, Cumin and Coriander or filfel chuma (optional)
- Salt and pepper, to taste
- 2 cups (320 g) cooked chickpeas, drained
- 4 white fish fillets (5–6 oz [140–168 g] each)
- Chopped fresh cilantro

Directions:

In a skillet, heat 1/3 cup of the oil on med-high heat. Once the oil is hot, add the bell peppers. Let the peppers blister and soften for about 20 minutes. Add the garlic and sauté for 2 minutes. Add the tomato paste and stir well, almost melting the paste into the peppers. Add the water, chile peppers, paprika, cumin, harissa (if using), salt and pepper. Mix well and let the paprika melt into the liquids. Taste and adjust the salt and pepper.

Add the chickpeas and place the fillets in the sauce. Cover and simmer for about 30 minutes, or until the fish is cooked and the sauce is reduced. Turn off the heat and sprinkle with the cilantro. Cover for 5 minutes. Serve.

Egyptian Goulash

Egyptian goulash consists of a meat and spinach filling in phyllo sheets.

Makes: 6 servings

Prep: 25 mins

Cook: 20 mins

Ingredients:

- 2 tbsp. olive oil, plus ½ tsp. for oiling
- 8 scallions, coarsely chopped
- 2 (10-ounce) packages fresh spinach, coarsely chopped
- 1 egg, beaten
- 1 cup crumbled feta cheese
- ½ tsp. freshly grated nutmeg
- Pinch of sea salt flakes
- Pinch of pepper
- 4 tbsp. butter
- 6 sheets of phyllo pastry
- 1 tbsp. sesame seeds

Directions:

Preheat the oven to 400°F. Brush a baking sheet with the ½ teaspoon of oil.

Heat the oil in a wok or large skillet over medium heat. Add the scallions and sauté for 1–2 minutes. Add the spinach and sauté for 3–4 minutes. Drain off any liquid and let cool slightly.

Stir the egg, feta, nutmeg, salt, and pepper into the spinach mixture. Melt the butter in a small saucepan.

Brush three sheets of phyllo with some of the melted butter. Place another sheet on top of each one and brush with more melted butter. Cut each pair of sheets down the middle to make six long strips in total. Place a tbsp. of the spinach filling on the end of each strip.

Lift one corner of phyllo over the filling to the opposite side, then turn over the opposite way to enclose. Continue to fold over along the length of the strip to make a triangular package, finishing with the seam underneath.

Place the packages on the prepared baking sheet, brush with the remaining melted butter, and sprinkle with sesame seeds. Bake for 12–15 mins. Serve hot.

Lamb Zucchini Goulash

A simple goulash recipe with lamb, zucchini and tomatoes.

Makes: 4 servings

Prep: 5 mins

Cook: 35 mins

Ingredients:

- 4-8 lamb chops
- Salt and pepper
- 2 tbsp. olive oil
- 1 onion, chopped finely
- 1 garlic clove, chopped finely
- 4 tbsp. ouzo (optional)
- 14 oz. canned tomatoes in juice
- Pinch of sugar
- ½ tsp. paprika
- 9 oz. zucchini, sliced
- 2 tbsp. chopped fresh thyme

Directions:

Season the lamb chops with pepper. Heat the oil in a flameproof casserole. Add in the onion and garlic. Cook for 5 minutes or until softened. Add the lamb chops and until browned on both sides.

Add the tomatoes with their juice, paprika, sugar, thyme and salt.

Boil and then simmer for 30 mins. stirring occasionally and turning the chops once during cooking, until the lamb and zucchini are tender.

Serve hot.

Chickpea Goulash

A vegan goulash recipe with chickpeas and pasta.

Makes: 4 servings

Prep: 10 mins

Cook: 1 hr. 5 mins

Ingredients:

- 14 oz. canned chickpeas, drained and rinsed
- 1 tbsp. olive oil
- 1 ½ cup small pasta, cooked
- 2 fresh oregano sprigs
- 1 tbsp. tomato purée
- Juice of 1 lemon
- 1 tsp. red pepper flakes
- 1 small red onion, chopped

Directions:

In a pot, add olive oil and onion and cook for 4 mins. Add in the beans, puree, oregano, juice and red pepper flakes and cook for 2 mins. Add in the cooked pasta and cook for 2 mins more.

Serve.

Crockpot Vegan Goulash

Delicious vegan goulash made in the crockpot.

Makes: 6 servings

Prep: 10 mins

Cook: 4 hrs.

Ingredients:

- 2 14 oz. canned chickpeas, drained and rinsed
- 1 tbsp. vegetable oil
- 1 cup diced onions
- 1 cup diced carrots
- One 16-ounce can tomatoes
- 1 cup vegetable stock
- 1 tbsp. paprika
- 1½ tsp. salt
- ½ tsp. pepper
- ¼ tsp. ground cloves
- 1 tbsp. brown sugar
- 2 tbsp. rice flour
- ¼ cup water

Directions:

Place chickpeas in your electric pot. Add the carrots, tomatoes, stock, paprika, salt, pepper, cloves, and sugar. Combine the rice flour with the water and stir in. Cover and cook for 4 hrs. on LOW.

Serve.

Viennese Goulash

Viennese goulash is made with a whole lot of onions.

Makes: 4 servings

Prep: 10 mins

Cook: 2 ½ hrs.

Ingredients:

- 1.75 oz. lard
- 1 lb. sliced onions
- 1 garlic clove chopped
- ½ tbsp. tomato puree
- 1 tbsp. paprika
- ¾ tsp. hot paprika
- ¼ tsp. crushed caraway seeds
- ½ tsp. brown sugar
- ¾ tsp. salt
- Pepper, to taste
- 1 tsp. apple cider vinegar
- 1 ½ lb. stewing cubed beef
- ½ tbsp. parsley

Directions:

In a pot, add the lard and fry the onions until golden. Add the garlic and cook for 1 min and then add the remaining ingredients except for the beef and parsley. Cover with ½ liter of water.

Then, when comes to boil, add the beef and cook for 2 hrs. or until done. Serve with parsley on top.

Low-Carb Lamb Goulash

Delicious goulash with zucchini and meat.

Makes: 4 servings

Prep: 5 mins

Cook: 35 mins

Ingredients:

- 4-8 lamb chops
- Salt and pepper
- 2 tbsp. olive oil
- 1 onion, chopped finely
- 1 garlic clove, chopped finely
- 14 oz. canned tomatoes in juice
- ½ tsp. paprika
- 9 oz. zucchini, sliced
- 2 tbsp. chopped fresh thyme

Directions:

Season the lamb chops with pepper. Heat the oil in a flameproof casserole. Add in the onion and garlic. Cook for 5 minutes or until softened. Add the lamb chops and until browned on both sides.

Add the tomatoes with their juice, paprika, thyme and salt.

Boil and then simmer for 30 mins. Stirring occasionally and turning the chops once during cooking, until the lamb and zucchini are tender.

Serve hot.

Chicken Goulash

A juicy and delicious paprika chicken goulash recipe.

Makes: 8 servings

Prep: 5 mins

Cook: 55 mins

Ingredients:

- 2 lb. skinless chicken thighs fillets, chopped
- 1 onion, sliced
- ½ tbsp. seasoned flour
- 1 crushed garlic clove
- Olive oil
- ½ green pepper, diced
- ½ carrot, diced
- ¾ tbsp. paprika
- ½ tsp. caraway seeds
- ½ cup chicken stock
- ½ cup cherry tomatoes

Directions:

Mix the chicken with the flour.

Heat ½ tablespoon oil in a pan. Cook the chicken until golden. Remove and set aside.

In the same pan, add the garlic & vegetables except the bell pepper. Cook for 10 mins or until softened. Add the bell pepper. Cook for 5 mins.

Put the chicken back in and add the remaining ingredients. Cover and cook for 40 mins or until done.

Serve.

Texan Goulash

Delicious Texas-style goulash recipe with bacon dripping and ground beef.

Makes: 4 servings

Prep: 10 mins

Cook: 25 mins

Ingredients:

- 8 ounces elbow macaroni
- 1 tbsp. bacon drippings or vegetable oil
- 1 pound ground beef
- 1 clove garlic, minced
- 1 (15-ounce) can tomato sauce
- 1 yellow onion, chopped
- 1 tbsp. paprika or chili powder, homemade or store-bought
- Salt
- Sour cream, for garnish (optional)

Directions:

Bring a pot of water added with salt to boil. Add the macaroni and cook until al dente, following the instructions on the package.

In a skillet, heat the bacon drippings over medium-high heat. Add the beef & cook, breaking up the meat with the side of a wooden spoon or spatula, for 5 to 7 minutes, until the meat is browned. Add the onion & cook, for about 3 mins, until wilted. Add the garlic and continue to cook for about 1 minute, until the garlic is lightly cooked. Add the tomato sauce and paprika and season with salt. Stir well and cook, stirring occasionally, for about 15 minutes to blend the flavors.

When the macaroni is done, drain well. Divide the macaroni among dinner plates and spoon the goulash over the top.

Serve.

One-Pot Goulash

A simple, one-pot goulash for a warm and comforting meal with no fuss.

Makes: 12 servings

Prep: 30 mins

Cook: 1 hr. 30 mins

Ingredients:

- 4 onions
- ½ tsp. pepper
- 4 tsp. lard
- 4 tbsp. paprika
- 2 tsp. caraway seeds
- 4 cups beef broth
- 1 lb. stewing beef & cut into one inch cubes
- 2 cups diced tomatoes
- 2 tsp. salt

Directions:

In a big pot, melt the lard. Add in the onion and cook for 3 mins. Add in the seeds & paprika.

Add meat to the pot and cook for 4 mins. Add in a bit of broth to remove the brown bit from the bottom of the pot & then add in the remaining. Add in the tomatoes and seasoning. Bring to boil and then cover & simmer for 2 hrs. or until meat is tender. Serve.

Ground Lamb Goulash

Delicious goulash recipe with macaroni and ground lamb.

Makes: 4 servings

Prep: 10 mins

Cook: 25 mins

Ingredients:

- 8 ounces elbow macaroni
- 1 tbsp. bacon drippings or vegetable oil
- 1 pound ground lamb
- 1 yellow onion, chopped
- 1 clove garlic, minced
- 1 (15-ounce) can tomato sauce
- 1 tbsp. paprika or chili powder, homemade or store-bought
- Salt
- Sour cream, for garnish (optional)

Directions:

Bring a pot water to a boil. Add the macaroni & cook until al dente, following the instructions on the package.

In a skillet, heat the bacon drippings over medium-high heat. Add the lamb and cook, breaking up the meat with the side of a wooden spoon or spatula, for 5 to 7 minutes, until the meat is browned. Add the onion & cook, for about 3 mins, until wilted. Add the garlic & continue to cook for about 1 minute, until the garlic is lightly cooked. Add the tomato sauce and paprika and season with salt. Stir well and cook, stirring occasionally, for about 15 minutes to blend the flavors.

When the macaroni is done, drain well. Divide the macaroni among dinner plates and spoon the goulash over the top.

Sweet Potato Goulash Soup

A warm and delicious goulash soup recipe with beef and sweet potato.

Makes: 4 servings

Prep: 20 mins

Cook: 1 hr.

Ingredients:

- 2 tbsp. oil
- 2 large onions, sliced
- 6 garlic cloves, sliced
- 0.8 lb. stewing beef, diced finely
- 2 tsp. caraway seeds
- 4 tsp. paprika
- 2 cans chopped tomatoes
- 4 ½ cup beef stock
- 2 sweet potatoes, diced

Directions:

Heat oil in a pot. Add in the onions & garlic and cook for 6 mins. Add in the beef and cook until beef is browned. Add in the seeds, paprika, stock and tomatoes and cook on low for 35 mins.

Add in the sweet potato and cook for 25 mins or until tender.

Serve.

Conclusion

Well, there you go! 30 delicious goulash recipes for you. Make sure you give each recipe a chance and try them all out! And don't forget to share with your friends and family!

About the Author

Allie Allen developed her passion for the culinary arts at the tender age of five when she would help her mother cook for their large family of 8. Even back then, her family knew this would be more than a hobby for the young Allie and when she graduated from high school, she applied to cooking school in London. It had always been a dream of the young chef to study with some of Europe's best and she made it happen by attending the Chef Academy of London.

After graduation, Allie decided to bring her skills back to North America and open up her own restaurant. After 10 successful years as head chef and owner, she decided to sell her business and pursue other career avenues. This monumental decision led Allie to her true calling, teaching. She also started to write e-books for her students to study at home for practice. She is now the proud author of several e-books and gives private and semi-private cooking lessons to a range of students at all levels of experience.

Stay tuned for more from this dynamic chef and teacher when she releases more informative e-books on cooking and baking in the near future. Her work is infused with stores and anecdotes you will love!

Author's Afterthoughts

I can't tell you how grateful I am that you decided to read my book. My most heartfelt thanks that you took time out of your life to choose my work and I hope you find benefit within these pages.

There are so many books available today that offer similar content so that makes it even more humbling that you decided to buying mine.

Tell me what you thought! I am eager to hear your opinion and ideas on what you read as are others who are looking for a good book to buy. Leave a review on Amazon.com so others can benefit from your wisdom!

With much thanks,

Allie Allen

Printed in Great Britain
by Amazon